Almee

SPEAKS

Almee
SPEAKS

PATRICIA ANN KEENE

Cover and interior design by The Book Cover Whisperer:
OpenBookDesign.biz

Paperback
eBook

Printed in the United States of America

FIRST EDITION

Who? What? Where? We all have questions.

Wouldn't you love to have answers?

NOW!

FOREWORD

About a year ago, I was driving home from work and musing in my head what to do and what it was all about—and darn it, how I hated having PTSD about freeway driving (leftover from an accident a few years back). A voice answered my questions—not a verbal outside voice, mind you, but an inner voice that was different from my usual thoughts.

Oh, boy, now I was for sure losing my mind—right? And there was laughter like sweet bells giggling in my head. And so it started...conversations on my drives. One day, I asked, "Who are you?"

"I am you," was the answer, and with it came a flood of understanding like a download for which there are no words.

"I am ALL of you."

So many questions flooded my mind: How? Who? Why? *Really?*

After a few days, I said I wished to put a name to *you.* "Are you female? Male? What—"

Nope. None/ALL of that—no limitation.

"Okay—then may I have a name to call you by or to think of you?"

"Whatever you wish," came the laughing answer. (I get that all the time—kind laughter.)

"Okay, then shall I call you All of Me...Almee?"

Almee said, "Write a book called *Almee Speaks* by Patricia Keen."

So here we go....

Let go . . .

ALMEE SPEAKS

I am learning to let go and let Almee in….

Fractals are never too small and never too big; they always retain their character and never lose their shape. You (we) are like that. You (we) are the same: complete, timeless. However, you are but a tiny, minute thread of the tapestry that is all of you—and all that is. Interwoven, limitless, always seeking and creating, contributing to the kaleidoscope of all. Experience is what we all bring back.

Think of a globe—endless numbers and sizes all connected. Within each globe dangles an untold number of threads, all connected to the outside. These dangling threads are each lifetime's experiences as conduits to our eternal selves and ALL. ALL contributing, ALL creating…always.

What are you?

_____

_____

_____

_____

_____

_____

_____

_____

_____

_____

_____

_____

_____

_____

_____

_____

ALMEE
SPEAKS

More of what "you" are: You (we/ALL) are a line dropping into this bubble of reality, and as that line works its way back into the top of the "bubble" edge and rejoins the ALL, you bring the experiences, choices, and creative nuances of that home with you…and all the innumerable lines contribute as they reabsorb back in due time.

ReUnite—though never separate—and then share, complete, and go out again for endless and absolutely extraordinary continuations of more and more and more.

Time has no limits, no beginnings—just as, simply put, a circle has no beginning and no end. It is self-perpetuating—it is not linear, nor is it flat, nor holistic. It is never-ending, multi-dimensional…streaming all that is, was, and will be, always in motion, always adding and growing in experience, creative ventures, and knowledge.

There are no limitations—just harmonies, colorful beyond what words can express. You ALL (we) know it, exercise it, and are welcome back as we ascend through this tiny bit and re-enter the ALL of ourselves. We (you) joyfully contribute our bit of life, experience, and insight as we rejoice. And there is LOVE as only it can truly be expressed.

ALMEE SPEAKS

Are there multiple versions of me existing at the same time here on Earth?

Of course…there is no limit to how we experience and tend to our creative processes. No, you'll not usually run into yourself—and if you did, you just wouldn't realize it. In fact, we do it all the time.

There are endless versions of you and endless "others," but automatically, all lives and experiences are mixed together. ALL and YOU have the essence intertwined within you. (Almee is laughing here.) So no, your mom wasn't "you," but in the end, we are ALL together. And yes, always endless and growing.

You have been many places, many times, may versions (places outside Earth). There are no limits— none—to ANYTHING, anytime, anywhere…it's hard

5

to drop all the restrictions on this thread to understand that…but it's okay, because that's why you (we) are here now and again. TIME is just an illusion to give a certain context or framework to the creations of experience, which are a kaleidoscope of what we (you) do.

Yes—just do it! This is best represented in the way the stream of connections flows…ideas, jobs, experiences. All return to home. The day you were born is the day you go home—you just don't realize it, of course.

ALMEE SPEAKS

We all bring the light, and to have light, we need darkness to define it. It is neither good nor bad—that is something that is relative to the circumstances that are created and desired to be experienced. It is all shades of grey between the lines, and we paint the colors of our interactions. No matter what the ramifications of any ONE thing, it is always each PARTICULAR take on experience/understanding/memory that brings the nuance of creation back to the whole as we return to our wholeness and share the lives we have made and created together.

Just as a butterfly's wings contain a multitude of color bits to make up the patterns of its exquisite wings, so our lives and individual takes and understandings, always changing, bring light and color to the infinite creative processes of the ever-growing existences we call the infinite—All-me, you, I—together and separate, continuous and always new, fresh and in awe of discovery, understanding, creativity, good, "bad," and every possible shade in between and throughout.

The day we are "born" is the day we begin our "homecoming." Make it a journey of courage and love—it won't feel like that most of the time—but reflect on all those bits. They COLOR your butterfly wings, and no two beings are ever the same.

ALMEE
SPEAKS

What is love?

Love is the disempowerment of evil. Pure love is the essence of completeness—which does not take, but gives in all ways to the loved one as well as the loving one. It is an indescribable essence of all that is—the GLUE of existence and beyond.

It has no substance, but is substantial. You find it in a baby's laugh, in a grandfather's eyes—in all of nature, in all that is—complete, and without end.

LOVE has always been, and always will be, in all of us: I—me—ALL.

Love cannot be broken, but it can be manipulated, warped, recreated into multiple forms, even made into "anti-love," or evil.

It is all a matter of expression and how that is served.

There is no bad or good per se—only what we create. And that has no bounds, no laws, no end or beginning. Love brings us to "heaven" or "hell...." We create what we will to be. That is what we bring in our own particular life—our completeness and rejoining in full the wholeness of all. No experience or understanding is without merit. In the infinite circle of ALL, everyone, everything, every bit is precious and welcome. ALL is knowledge, understanding, and LOVE.

ALMEE SPEAKS

R isk. Why do we feel it, and what does it have to do with experience?

Risk is a perceived notion that can be used as a plus or minus feeling. It can drive the actions we take. What does that have to do with anything? It can stop you in your tracks or propel you onward.

Risk is the perceived danger that something of value can be lost or removed. Even gained knowledge presents a risk, because with it, a different idea, or a reduction in ignorance or innocence, can be lost.

Without RISK, there is little to be gained. When we create anything, there is always the chance it could destroy us or what we have created before. Keep in mind that time is an illusion; therefore, all things are always at play, always maneuvering. Every possibility is in the works simply to be experienced and brought into the continuing collection of creation—and, in so doing, it is recreated all over again, always the same and always new.

Risk lets us know that we are touching that creativity.

ALMEE SPEAKS

Connectivity is something all of us have in common—always, we are intermingled—but in this space, we can obtain the illusion of separation and selfhood that allows us to paint the experiences we bring to our lifetimes. Even here, we gravitate toward togetherness, as that is our nature. Solitude is something we can create, experience, and include as we complete our reunion.

In the quiet of this experience, there is a resonance of that which makes us unique, always, even in our intertwining. A spark of selfhood flashes with unique insights and longings that propel us in our creative endeavors.

Without quiet, there is no noise, no reason to clap or sing or laugh or wonder. In loneliness, we drive ourselves. We search for meaning and listen for all the things we wish to know...to understand every facet, every fractal, every NEW bit of wonder.

All of us—me, I, you—we celebrate the wonderful colors of it all. Always a new perspective, a new under-standing...without end, ever growing and changing, spectacular in the way that no two clouds or sunsets are ever the same....

ALMEE SPEAKS

Where do we come from? Wherever you are is where you have always been. It is the artifacts and the things and experiences we create that change around us.

Before "birth," you were present and in communication with the eternal NOW. As you know, time is an illusion, a construct upon which to place relevant created experiences.

There are many ways to describe "before," if you will, but understand that it is always the present, whether you realize it or not. We are always interacting and subconsciously aware of our completeness. We have chosen to make things simple by closing our memories of home into the particular experience we choose in this creation (this life).

Sometimes, bits and flashes leak through. These are interpreted in many ways: "past lives," Heaven, etc. All things exist simultaneously; we recreate them over and over, and the ALL comes into play.

It's a bit like knowing the steps to a dance; as we perform them, we adjust, we improvise. And we recreate all the dances…always.

ALMEE SPEAKS

Thought. Where does it come from? Why do we have a sense of self?

Self is our anchor to the reality we are experiencing and creating—otherwise, we would be lost in the onslaught of incoming reactions to and feelings about our world, our experiences, and our PLACE in all we perceive.

If you cannot be in the moment of selfhood, you drift, you lose contact—sometimes just briefly—with the moment. For example, when you drive a well-known route to work every day and perhaps lose yourself in inner thoughts or music—all of a sudden, you've gotten from point A to point B, and you didn't even notice. Where were you? Yes, it is almost as if you were out of body. In a way, you were....

So, when you get lost in thought, or a great book or experience, you pull anchor and FLY above it all. We (you, I, we) are not just a body. The body is a vessel that allows us a bit of disconnection from the allness of what we truly are, to bring a separate and distinct accent of creation back to ALL. Our inner musings allow that ANCHOR to settle us momentarily in order to receive and perhaps process and push forward that creative mystery we love: self.

ALMEE SPEAKS

F eelings. When and why do we have them? In our life, we interpret and interact within our sphere of sensations. "Feelings" such as sadness, happiness, etc. are the chemical interactions our bodies put forth to "stamp" a particular range of memories within our body. It runs the gamut. Crying is known to release stress and/or heighten feelings of joy…and then we connect to our higher selves as this happens. This "stamp," if you will, helps us in our negotiations through life. (We aren't the only beings to do this.)

Complex interrelationships are the most intriguing and creative—like a symphony of many sounds to create beautiful and heartfelt music. "Feelings" have many "colors." The vibration of creation is not just one

CHORD or one COLOR—it weaves, dances, and sings in all kinds of ways through all dimensions.

Embrace your "feelings:" good, bad, and everything in between. Explore them, play with them. They help form the texture of the creative process. It all comes full circle as we reunite, each life returning to the ALL....

ALMEE SPEAKS

F ear is usable if you embrace it and redirect the energy coming your way. You are hardwired to experience the chemical releases brought by emotion, but as we all know, fear can be misplaced and become something that hinders us, something that is not helpful.

Breathe, breathe, breathe—take a moment to find out what that feeling is telling you. Do you need to run from actual danger, or is there another reason?

Sometimes, an inner burst of energy is just that! It's energy—like walking out in front of people to speak, or perhaps an old memory that can no longer really hurt you. Mold the energy. Hold it close and release it in a big joyful breath.

Our bodies process fear from eons of ancestors and human development. It serves many purposes. Doing something new can provoke fear, but that's okay. You are just being reminded that you may be pushing an envelope worth pushing.

Take the many nuances of "fear" and create within them.

ALMEE SPEAKS

*S*uccess is always something we look for…but what is it, really? It's subjective, for sure…once we define a particular goal, only then can we identify what "success" means to us in that moment.

Just going through your thoughts and finding out what something means doesn't necessarily bring closure. Flexibility is paramount to the journey.

As we evolve our outlook and take aim at certain aspects of what we think would equate to "success," keep in mind that it isn't just "reaching" the goal that's important, but how the process makes us feel as it moves forward. There is no LACK of success if, for example, we need to recalibrate the "GOAL" midstream. We find success in the PROCESS.

Remember, it's okay to not reach that goal…you

will become successful by looking forward and understanding the reasons why. We continue to grow and create, and that, my friends, is what "SUCCESS" is all about.

ALMEE SPEAKS

Thanksgiving Day

Giving thanks brings us to eternity! We are infinite, never-ending, creative, and compassionate by nature, but giving thanks nurtures us and combines us in ways we may have forgotten.

A moment of grace percolates through us as we feel gratitude—thankful to realize what we have, who we are, and what we can do.

There is no better feeling than gratitude. It brings in the love and clarity of our creations, connections, and humanity.

We can be thankful for BIG and tiny things…anything. We can EVEN be thankful for being thankful… as we recognize what it is, and how lovely it is to feel the WARMTH of that moment.

Move it forward, open all your senses. Even in sadness, we can be grateful, for if we had nothing, we could never feel loss.

Painting with all the COLORS gives us every opportunity to create awesome possibilities. Thankfulness glues all those bits together.

ALMEE SPEAKS

ntolerance is a "festering" within you. Intolerance "inside" takes its toll on the one who chooses to demonstrate this side of themselves. We can all harbor it—but why do we allow it? FEAR. That's what stokes intolerance.

Fear of something different, something unfamiliar, something you don't understand. Why on Earth would you let such a thing rule you? There is no reason anyone with an open mind should ever harbor such a state.

No, you need not tolerate anything that can HARM or promote HARM—but be available to opening your heart, your eyes, your mind to other things. Don't be so selfish as to hold onto narrow minded, non-inclusive beliefs, as this not only destroys you but kills the creative process, as well. FEAR NOT. Look with an open mind and heart. Create with an open mind and heart.

Intolerance pulls us inward and does not let us BLOOM. Our gardens must have many different colors, many different plants. DIFFERENCE is diversity; diversity is growth. And growth brings us much, much more.

ALMEE
SPEAKS

S ecurity brings to mind a multitude of ideas. What does it feel like, and why do we seek it?

Feeling secure anchors you/us. It puts the soul at ease. When we feel secure, we are grounded in our reality so we can venture out freely without any nagging fears.

You can create a feeling of security at any time. It's not something that comes to you, but something that comes FROM you.

And yes, of course, there are circumstances that will push you in many ways. Reach inside, if even for a moment; breathe deep and reach up to your most creative wholeness. Pull down your moment of groundedness. Build on that. As you cultivate this habit, you will create an inner security within, knowing in the moment that you are complete, you are infinite, and there is NOTHING more you need.

You may go in many directions, as is our habit in life, but you can always reach for your SECURITY blanket whenever you wish…you just have to put yourself there.

ALMEE SPEAKS

The world in which we live lives in us. Our environment depends on the good graces of our stewardship. We don't get it, of course; but lessons are being sent, and shall be learned. Humans don't realize how powerful they are. Great power must also be tempered with great courage and understanding. We are only just beginning to REALLY see that. Yes, the damage has been done, but absolutely nothing is SET forever. Feel our Earth, feel yourselves, feel all the living and non-living things. Wrap them around your heart and soul, and KNOW you are the co-creators as well as the destroyers. So is everything else we create together and as one.

Nothing is lost, BAD, or wrong, as long as we learn and find better ways—good, creative, useful ways.

31

Open your eyes and SEE. It is so easy to continue to be blind. Be LOVING in all things!

ALMEE
SPEAKS

W hat about when we "don't know?" That is a pretty open idea. Not knowing is a bit of a hallmark of living this life. It's in the "not knowing" that you learn to know. Why (and how) is this?

When you realize the essence that you already KNOW, but do not remember, there is a cathartic release that must happen in order to accept that. Embrace this, and rejoice in the PROCESS of rediscovery and the creation of new experiences. To understand something that was once a mystery is exhilarating, and brings out our true purpose: to fully see with these eyes, this heart, and this experience, as it is always unique and precious.

Sometimes this can be heartbreaking, but it is all a part of us. A well-rounded life continually seeks the creative process in so many ways—not always as we wish, but the glory is in the learning, the understanding that comes with it. So many infinite possibilities, and every ONE has meaning. We force our collective "knowing" by starting with a blank page—NOT knowing—and we blossom from there.

ALMEE
SPEAKS

P roductive creation is balanced by destructive creation. What we do to produce something can be undone; this is normal and not to be confused with evil or bad things.

The way of nature is thus balanced, as all energies and intentions cycle around each other and fill the gaps in all things. Creative endeavors are multidimensional and interdimensional.

Everything already exists in matter/antimatter and other forms of energy. We just manipulate that in infinite ways to "produce" want—or, for that matter, what we don't want. In this way, whatever you put your mind to can be manipulated or "created." That goes for many realms, whether in thought or physical form.

So yes, we are masters of ALL in many ways, but

we are tasked with limitations on memory and skills so that in our DISCOVERIES, we find "aknew" (new) facets of creation we can share and wonder at. Thus, the magic of that wondrous moment is forever included in our creative sharing, both productive and "destructive."

ALMEE SPEAKS

Dimensions are a bit tricky to describe in the limited language at hand, but here it "grows" (goes):

We have control over three dimensions as well as east/west and north/south.

The 4th dimension includes the above, plus time (control of past, present, and future).

The 5th dimension includes all of the above, plus control of the current/present body timeline with respect to "aging." You can stay the same, grow younger, older, up/down as you wish while maintaining your current body.

There are many more dimensions as well as possibilities—an infinite number, to be exact, that allow different experiences to play out.

Of course, when you "return" to your wholeness,

none of that is needed—you have already processed the complete creative collective of possibilities.

Breaking it down to simple truths brings newness to the experience, and that is what we love to bring back into the field of ALL, thereby adding to the never-ending tapestry of creation. Our completeness is defined, celebrated, and shared…and we are inspired and grow always forward to expand our oneness of love….

ALMEE SPEAKS

"**P**eace on Earth."

When we feel peace, there is a wonderful awareness of settlement, comfort, and belonging. This is something we feel from the beginning, even at conception. The ability to recreate…that is a blessing for yourself as well as those around you.

Clarity of heart and mind slow the life processes down and allow us to truly maneuver and create within a loving space. We are always in search of that connection and clarity.

"Peace on Earth" is not just for this time of year—it is vital anytime. Throughout Earth's history, there have been upheavals and peace, for humanity and nature alike. There have been many epochs through time that humanity has forgotten, and we move forward over and over again. This is something we do—in addition to other experiences in other places. Like waves on the ocean, we move up and down, and peace is the glassy, smooth water where we can rest and reflect, perhaps seeing clearly for one day, then learning to move forward....

ALMEE SPEAKS

All is one, and one is all. We are always aware of the fact that we are more than meets the eye...not consciously most of the time, but with a deep understanding, a longing that draws us onward and inward.

There is no end to our connections—now, in the past, or in the future. We extend into many realms. Our "brains" tend to limit the knowledge and abilities that would otherwise allow us to create meaning in small (but mighty) ways.

Stopping to smell the roses is so very crucial, as the glory of ALL is highlighted in moments of profound and suspended delight and awareness. In one moment of "delight," all that we are is revealed: always creative, always in awe, and, even if just for a moment, beyond all that is.

Sometimes, we feel very small, very unintentional—but in embracing that "beat," we encompass how big and endless we truly are. We are always united, always complete, no matter what the moment might bring.

ALMEE
SPEAKS

New beginnings. Every moment is a new beginning, a fresh perspective, a new outlook. Once again, all is new, ever-changing, forever new. Just contemplating change creates a window in your mind. Your creative urge pushes out with joy.

You can never fail if you never try—and if you never try, you will never know the joy of creation. We are not meant to be stagnant. We wallow and die in stagnation, whether from fear, laziness, or any other reason under the sun. The process of life—living—is just that…a process.

The act of breathing is a lovely reminder of how it all works. Breathing is unconscious, but it can be conscious when we wish it to be. Life is also conscious if we wish it to be…or unconscious. Every moment, AWAKE or asleep, is a new moment, a new beginning. We roll onward, outward, upward—but we ROLL ON. All things continue, whether living or not.

ALL new beginnings create the infinite, and the infinite is always now.

ALMEE SPEAKS

Joy and compassion are the yin and yang of life.

Compassion creates joy, and joys reaches all the nooks and crannies of our emotions.

We are just a dot, but we are infinite in our ability to become infinite. Joy is a learned expression of our human state. We are "joy-ful" when we are full of joy. We create this when we connect with others. Without connection, we wither and die, both literally and spiritually.

Compassion allows us to grow and connect with others. We were never meant to be alone—for even in solitude, we are always in connection. Our connections bridge all things, allowing the joy of love to permeate ALL. And the joy of love and gratitude and creative rebirth, day in and day out, is what makes us wise, forever fluid and permeable.

As you negotiate your particular road in life, remember that your journey will always lead back to the infinite and to love, bringing your own unique spin on life—and that is joyful.

ALMEE SPEAKS

When disappointment and chaos rule—just breathe. Count every second and every molecule passing in and out, in and out. We can thrive under such circumstances if we suspend fear.

Disappointment can only stop you if you allow EXPECTATIONS to override your true sense of self. Stop and look inward. Know that you truly have this—if not today, then someday. It may not be in the cards, but only so it doesn't keep you down. Flow, flow, flow—roll forward when you fall, and shake it off. Embrace yourself. You will prevail.

CHAOS is only a medium for lots of energy running amuck. Embrace it and flow, flow, flow. Like the ocean, we are all a part of the bigger picture; we just tend to forget that. Move with the energy. Out of chaos come order, creativity, and surprises. We have all we need. We don't need to hold on too tightly. Let a little chaos out and watch the fun begin....

ALMEE SPEAKS

Friendship. Friends. We are all together in all ways. We separate in order to create clean, clear experiences and bring back something unique. No two beings are in any way the same, even if they appear so. Nothing is in the same experience or born from exactly the same understanding. We all COLOR our experiences differently.

Friendship is support and sharing of all of this, and it is a very human way to share as we understand things in the moment. We can communicate and compare notes, support and celebrate ourselves.

Friends are like the SPICES we include in our own particular recipe of life. We bring all sorts of love and comfort to ourselves as we maneuver through our journeys. Friendship echoes our infinite relationships as we reconnect and bring back our creative experiences. We revel in all of our intertwined collaborations, intentional or unintentional. Life is just that—joyous, creative collaborations of creation. Sometimes, it takes a village....

ALMEE SPEAKS

L ife is short, and it is meant to be so. This is so we can create value and meaning along the way. If we were long-lived, there would be a slowing of activity, as if there were no end, no reason to lift a finger.

Of course, things are perceived as relative; we create the meaning that was meant to be. Creation and life are always a joy, and joyful things cannot just squander time. Precious is that which is fleeting and tangible in the blink of an eye. The clouds in the sky are always changing, never exactly the same—beautiful, unique, and always moving.

Our lives are also unique, always moving, always beautiful and never exactly the same. This is precious. That which is impermanent—what we cannot hold onto—is, in its moment, joyful. It is special, always and forever; it is to be embraced, cherished. All life is short, but infinite in joy and creation.

ALMEE SPEAKS

What is reality? What is truth?

When do you feel at home in yourself? Is it when the truth of reality feels right? We all know that feeling: when you are comfortable in your own skin and what you have before you rings true, even if just for a moment.

The truth of truth lies within us, always present but at the same time elusive; it is something we are drawn to seek, for it is never still.

As reality shifts and becomes what we make it in any given moment, so does truth. My truth is not necessarily your truth, but somehow, we all recognize it. We all come out of love and truth. As we create our current lives, we pull this into our creative process, our "reality."

To be in the moment…settled and alert, with no judgment…now you are home.

Truth, home, reality—always with us, always changeable, unique, and limitless, grounded and creative. We are always at home in love. Feel it—be it. Yes!

ALMEE
SPEAKS

Vulnerability.

Yes, we all feel the vulnerability of our lives. We can feel that moment of helplessness, of being in a very scary place. It is one of the most human (and humane) parts of ourselves. We can relate to all things in such moments. Here today—gone tomorrow.

Why do we need to have such helplessness built in at times? It softens us and allows us to meld with all things. Not just living, as you understand it—but all things as we traverse our presence in this life. Earth, the universe, the tiniest of subatomic particles: we are all vulnerable—all at risk, if you will—and that is precious beyond all things. In that very scared place comes new and unknown creation. To not know brings forth astonishment and delight, but we must be open and pliable in order to feel it…soft and yielding, vulnerable enough to be swayed, to be transformed. Do not harden yourself; flow and transform. Find the ultimate joy in vulnerability.

ALMEE SPEAKS

I got cold feet today, and held off—I have no idea why. When you don't believe in yourself, it can stop you in your tracks. Case in point: Was I feeling like a fraud? Was I just empty? I was frozen, but sometimes we just have to pick up the pen and let it go in faith that something—anything—will commence and come forth.

Being human is tricky. It doesn't come with a set of instructions. And that is exactly what is supposed to happen. Just show up and follow your gut, be present, be in that moment. You push the fear away by filling up your moments, one step at a time. You don't have to know where you're going, or how you'll get there—but you will. The capacity we have for our creative process is endless and forever running in our very soul...so believe, and so it shall be. Jump in with both feet and keep rolling forward—you will surprise yourself and light up the way!

ALMEE
SPEAKS

Let it flow. Look deep inside yourself and transform from the inside out. ALL is out there, and all is within us.

We are never lacking—only so much as we allow ourselves to accept that conclusion. To lack is to want. If you don't feel complete, it is as though you are broken and unable to function. This, of course, is not true. We choose to do so, whether consciously or unconsciously.

We are always complete, always perfect—even if our body is not. Our infinite selves are always there, like the phantom missing limb. We are complete in ways we just don't remember; that is part of being human and experiencing this creative endeavor.

You can always feel assured that you are complete, and in every way perfect for all things. Let not the negative overwhelm you—feel it, acknowledge it, and let it pass on by. We are all endless: infinite and never alone, connected and complete.

ALMEE SPEAKS

Self-worth is something we all wonder about. We are all priceless, but it is the nature of life to discover that. To do so means allowing gaps and holes to fill the once-complete picture of our feeling of worthiness.

Why? What could the purpose be of something so toxic and demeaning as the loss of our own worthiness? It opens up areas to reestablish new and valuable means of creation. Fine-tuning ourselves in this way, we go forward and are never-ending, always renewing. When we find that nugget of self-worth, we feel renewed, recreated.

Worth implies that there is value or something worth protecting. Worth is more than just "being."

Know this: We are all worthy, complete, and infinitely priceless.

Never fear that you/we/us are "less than." We are perfect and endlessly valuable.

ALMEE SPEAKS

A vatars come in many forms. Your current body is an avatar of sorts. It allows a part of you to interact in this realm, and is discarded at some point in "death."

Other beings from different parts of the galaxy will also use an avatar when exploring space. They remain safe in their environment, but can upload themselves into an artificial body that is disposable if need be. These bodies are quite advanced with many senses. Like a video game, they allow the experiences and interaction needed to function in hazardous environments or conditions, and they need no upkeep. If something unwanted were to happen, these beings are capable of simply vacating to an avatar. An interesting thing about the avatars of some groups is that they can withstand travel when (and where) a living being could not, whether though space, time, or other dimensions.

Humans are simple at this time, but we interact with avatars all the time without knowing it. Your experiences in this reality are uncomplicated by design and infinitely worthy by creation.

ALMEE
SPEAKS

S o, where do we go from here? How do we overcome our inner fears and anxieties?

Breathe, breathe, breathe. First of all, any fears you carry around within yourself are of your own manufacture, even if they are based at some time in actual events. No matter what the root cause, they mustn't poison your ability to think and function as you wish.

Over time, we can stock away a lot of unconscious fears. So, how to rid ourselves of them? How can we even know what they are?

When you feel inner turmoil and unknown dread (or even known dread), take a moment to NOT push it away. Stop, embrace it fully, and encompass it within your whole being for a moment. Validate the feeling and breathe it out. Let it dissipate and disappear. Exhale. Do this you're in a calm and settled moment. Do not fear the fear. Be open and compassionate to yourself. We all create fears, and we all create love. It is an ongoing process and part of who we are.

ALMEE SPEAKS

A re our lives written in the stars? Yes and no. We orchestrate how we choose to experience our life, but we have no control over the path it takes. Sounds odd, doesn't it?

ALL that we are is focused from the inside out; but with that, we are also on an arranged sub-status, if you will. The stage is set, and now the actors manipulate the ways in which various narratives will run due course within any given "play." There are infinite stages and infinite plays going on all at the same time.

So, yes and no. We are the creative muses of our own lives, experiences, and how all of that weaves itself into the ongoing tapestry of all that is, was, and will be. For what is certain is that nothing will ever be exactly the same, even if that means just one atom, or one perception, or even just looking and seeing the difference from many angles, ever-evolving in endless and predetermined creation.

ALMEE SPEAKS

When you feel beyond down and heavy with life's issues, stop, pause, and settle yourself. Picture your core as a glowing orb of light—see that orb spinning faster and faster. As it spins, the "plaque" of whatever is holding you back will fly off and disappear. You can do this anytime for any reason. Unload from your being anything that is clinging to you. You are lighter and brighter; you can expand like a breath of fresh air.

We are so very good at creating; we can bring in the light or leave the darkness. There is nothing wrong with either, unless you feel burdened by that which you simply don't want. We are endless and always in motion, so feel that. Let it sink into all you do. When we celebrate ourselves, we celebrate all of us and all of what we are.

So, spin away and shine. Be bright, be light, be connected to all you/we are.

ALMEE SPEAKS

Today we are talking about the wind. Because when travel happens, physical or otherwise, we move through invisible forces.

Vital is the wind we ride on, vital is the wind we push against. It propels us and repels us. Without it, there is no definition or dimension to our travels.

Through life, we push and pull the wind. Through all that is, we create definition through interaction. We are not, unto ourselves, singular. We exist throughout all things, even if we cannot see or feel it.

The invisible wind shows itself by what it DOES; we show ourselves by what we do, by how we make others feel. That elusive emotion defines us.

Making ourselves felt connects us to each other in

deep, tangible, endless ways. As we travel, the wind uplifts us, propels us, connects us and allows us to be felt.

As a sweet breeze gently caresses your senses... embrace the wind.

ALMEE SPEAKS

"**A**I" is in the news, and with it a fear-based message.

We often default to fear in the face of what we don't understand. Should there be fear here? Is AI a danger to us? No; it is not to be feared. Yes, it is to be understood, and to be part of us.

We created this. It is a glorious extension of us, but in our embracing of it, we must also understand its far-reaching possibilities, and that shouldn't destroy our creative ability to flow and go with it. As we continue to expand and move into our future, many things may happen. We are adaptable and must keep an open mind...and open eyes.

If things are not what we are comfortable with, then we can adjust them—but there is no need to destroy everything. Take what is good and useful, and be willing to put aside that which is not. Keep the creative juices flowing. Don't let FEAR freeze us into inaction or destruction.

Slow down and breathe. Look at things, and really let all possibilities become lit so that we can always move forward, expanding and embracing our creative and best selves.

ALMEE SPEAKS

S tepping out one step at a time…moving forward grows our intent to remain in this plane. If we only dwell in the past, we stop living; we die, both mentally and physically. Dream of what you want to do, big or small—but look forward. Make plans, make movement. Discover new and exciting things. Just because you have "years" doesn't mean your expiration date is up next. No matter what the situation at hand, even the smallest forward peek is what keeps us vibrant and engaged in life. We may not "control" our outcomes or what happens around us, but we will always have our most important part—our endlessness, and our total connection to all that is, was, and will be.

So be unafraid. Be curious, be loving and happy. Why not? No matter what, each tiny bit is precious, never to be exactly the same again. Take notice; pay attention,

whether "good" or "bad…."

ALMEE
SPEAKS

W e are isolates in this experience, but when we die, we reunite as one with all.

You are still you, but now all the experiences within you are shared, understood, cherished, and enhanced by the common communication and love of all, and they with you.

No matter who you are or what you do, your creative lifetime, be it long or short, adds to the infinite and eternal oneness and celebration of all.

It is a great sacrifice to be separated from the love and support of the many to be isolated in the experience of this type of life. We are always looking for understanding and connection, as is our nature. But to truly bring specialness to this creation, we must bring a new and completely separate spin to our eyes and what we say, do, and understand.

With joy and excitement, we will rejoin in full, bringing our unique and precious life's adventures with us as we rejoin all of who we are.

AUTHOR BIO

PATRICIA KEENE lives in Tucson, Arizona. Worked in Medicine as a Radiographer, Researcher, Radiation Therapist for 30 years. Also worked with animals as a Veterinary Tech. Has had all kinds of critters: from mice to horses. Loves to do acting, selling, traveling— and anything else that comes along.

Made in the USA
Las Vegas, NV
16 November 2023

80967696R00052